# Explore Your Creativity With Mandalas Coloring Book

## Art Exploration With Mandalas Coloring Book

Mandala Coloring Book

By : Gala Publication

2

Published By :

Gala Publication
© Copyright 2015 – Gala Publication

ISBN-13: **978-1522708032**
ISBN-10: **1522708030**

# Design 1

# Design 2

# Design 3

# Design 4

7

# Design 5

# Design 6

# Design 7

# Design 8

# Design 9

# Design 10

# Design 11

# Design 12

# Design 13

# Design 14

# Design 15

# Design 16

# Design 17

# Design 18

# Design 19

# Design 20

# Design 21

# Design 22

# Design 23

# Design 24

# Design 25

# Design 26

# Design 27

# Design 28

# Design 29

# Design 30